THE ALL NEW STYLE OF MAGAZINE-BOOKS

SDM LIVE ®

www.SDMLIVE.com

MP

MOCY PUBLISHING
WWW.MOCYPUBLISHING.COM

Printed by CreateSpace, An Amazon.com Company

SDM LIVE®

EDITOR-IN-CHIEF
D. "Casino" Bailey
casino@sdmlive.com

EDITORIAL DIRECTOR
Sheree Cranford
sheree@sdmlive.com

GRAPHIC/WEB DESIGNER
D. "Casino" Bailey
casino@sdmlive.com

ACCOUNT EXECUTIVE
Frank Harvest Jr.
frank@sdmlive.com

PHOTOGRAPHERS
Anterlon Terrell Fritz
Treagen Colston
Terance Drake

CONTRIBUTORS
April Smiley
Courtney Benjamin

COPY ORDERS & ADVERTISING OFFICE
Send Money Order or Check to:
Mocy Publishing
P.O. Box 35195
Detroit, Michigan 48235
(586) 646-8505
advertise@sdmlive.com

Copy Order Item
SDM Live Magazine Issue #17
S&H Plus Retail Price - $9.99 per copy

WWW.SDMLIVE.COM

Printed by CreateSpace, An Amazon.com Company

MP
MOCY PUBLISHING

Copyright © 2017 Support Detroit Movement,
a division of Mocy Music Publishing, LLC and
C'Cliche, LLC. All rights reserved.
Printed in the U.S.A.

REAL MUSIC. REAL ENTERTAINMENT.®

SDM LIVE®

ISSUE 17

ALSO
ESKO
JAMAL
ALLEN SR.
CHRIS
OCTOBER
JORDAN
RIVER
SHARIEK
L'ZZZ
KAY
JANEY

RASHELLE REY
AWARD WINNING STAGE
PLAY AND BOOK AUTHOR

JP ONE
WRITES A LETTER TO HIS
FANS ABOUT HIS LOCKUP

JARAY
R&B SENSATION
BACK WITH A HIT

WWW.SDMLIVE.COM

ISSUE 17 - 2017

CONTENTS

pg. 12
JARAY
ready to sing and
dance down the
biggest stage possible

pg. 16
RASHELLE REY
is on a mission
to use her gifts
to heel the world

pg. 20
JESUS ESKO
in the works
of a major move
and a new deal

pg. 23
TOP 10 CHARTS
The hottest albums
and digital singles
this month features
Cardi B., King Dillon,
DJ Kahled and more.

1

Nintendo - Switch™ 32GB Console - Gray Joy-Con™
$299.99
www.bestbuy.com

2

Bose® - QuietComfort® 35 wireless headphones - Black
$329.99
www.bestbuy.com

3

Samsung - Galaxy View - 18.4" - 32GB - Black
$399.99
www.bestbuy.com

Raising The Bar

THE HOTTEST AWARD SHOW OF 2017 LEFT A LASTING IMPRESSION ON THE ENTERTAINMENT WORLD IN THE CITY OF DETROIT

by Cheraee C.

There have been a rise in Detroit of award shows paying homage to Detroit artists, but none of them can top the 2017 SDM Live Awards. SDM Live had the red carpet laid out accented with the SDM Live backdrop, attendees were dressed to impress in their most classiest attire, and the visuals were bananas. The 2017 SDM Live Awards were August 5, 2017 at Marygrove College. Winners who took home the gold were Jp One, Gucci Rie, Big Gov, Pierre Anthony, Dj Steady Rock, 7 Mile Radio, Mula Films, and a few others. The lovely 3xotic opened the show with a phenomenal performance followed by JaRay, King Dillon, Prince Dee, Katrina Carson, Queen Bre, Esko, and many more who also shut down the stage. It was nothing, but positive vibes and a positive ambience throughout the award show. If you missed the 2017 SDM Live Awards, stay tuned for the awards next year.

Crude Affiliation

URBAN FICTION WRITER AND DETROIT NATIVE L.L MARIE GETS NITTY AND GRITTY WITH HER NEW BOOK RELEASE

by Cheraee C.

Detroit's own L.L Marie was on a literary mission when she wrote her debut novel *Crude Affiliation* Chronicles. You never know what different affiliations can lead you too.

This 617 page urban thriller is super descriptive from the first sentence to the last chapter. Each and every memory, experience, and scene is expressed to the fullest extent showing realism and sym-bolism. If you don't know anything about Detroit or want to know what it's like to come up in Detroit you will after reading this book.

As a mother and her five sons Ray, Sway, Cent, Ronnie, and Lester each high-light their lives from boy to men, from the streets to the sheets, you are in for a page-turning journey.

Crude Affiliation
By L.L Marie

Available from Amazon.com and other online stores

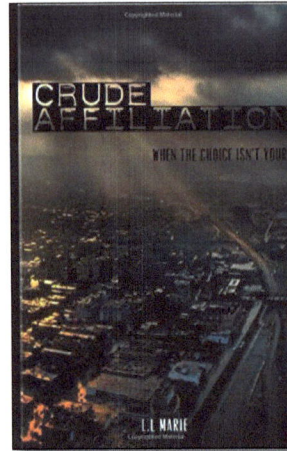

FUNDS2HELP
MAKING A CHANGE TOGETHER

Funds2Help.com is a place where people can get help with crowdfunding, business funding, personal funding and more. Funds are donated instantly to users Paypal account with no waiting time.

www.Funds2Help.com

Jiving and Raving

DETROIT RECORDING ARTIST JARAY SPEAKS ON PERFORMING AT THE SDM LIVE AWARDS AND THE LIFE OF BEING AN INDEPENDENT ARTIST

by Cheraee C.

Q. How does it feel to be performing at the 2017 SDM Live Awards and be nominated in multiple award categories?

A. I'm so amped up about performing! I don't really get to gig as much as I would like to so when I do get an opportunity like this, I take it very seriously and try to give a really memorable performance! I want to give the best performance I've ever had for this show! I can't wait! I was kind of shocked to be nominated in 3 categories. BUT I did work very hard to create my debut album and it feels good to get some type of recognition for my original music that I executive produced, wrote, and performed. Of course I have an extremely dope producer who I have give credit to for helping me make it happen. Shout out to Darell "Red" Campbell!

Q. Do you feel like your music career has been more successful with you being independent or working with a label? Why or why not?

A. I feel there are definitely advantages and disadvantages to working with a label and working as an independent artist. As an Indie Artist, I have control of everything. I make the final decisions... I wear all of the hats. There is a creative freedom that I appreciate and can't do without. However, working with a label and getting signed can be a great thing IF you get a good deal and the business end is solid. To answer the question, I think I have done well as an Indie Artist but I am not satisfied and don't feel I have reached the level at which I can be. I will continue to strive and do what I do, and hey, if the right opportunity comes along, who knows what could happen?

Q. Out of all the music artists you've opened up for, which artist/group did you enjoy opening up for the most?

A. Well, I guess I would say Mint Condition. Just being in the presence of legends, talented musicians... watching, absorbing the energy, and the professionalism was a great learning experience.

Q. Do you dedicate all your time to music, do you have a 9 to 5, and how do you utilize your spare time?

A. Unfortunately, as much as I would love to do music full time, it's not possible for me at this point in my life. I mean I have to pay bills! I need money to invest in myself... So, I work a full time job. I wish I had someone that would pay all my bills, let me live for free while I dedicated 100% of my time to music! That would be the life, right?

Q. If you could tell your fans one thing they don't know about JaRay what would it be?

A. Hmmm... Believe it or not... I am deathly shy of small crowds! Like I get so nervous when it comes to singing for small groups! I don't know why but, I do. I think it's the intimacy. the up close and personal of it. I'm fine when I'm on a stage kind of far away from the people.

Singing Is A Blessing

SONGWRITER AND SINGER CHRIS OCTOBER WEARS HIS MUSIC CAREER
ON HIS SLEEVES AND IS ON THE ROAD TO BEING NEXT LEVEL

by Cheraee C.

Q. How did you get started in the music industry?

A. Well I started out singing as a child in church, but in the game I started in a R&B group in Detroit and we did a lot. We were featured on BET's 106 and Park w.o.w.

Q. Where do you see your music career in the next three years?

A. I see my career next level in three years, selling records and touring mainly, and blessing communities because God blessed me.

Q. Do you feel like managers slow down your music career or advance it? Who's your current manager?

A. I feel like a good manager is valuable and critical to the longevity of the career, and my current manager name is Sarah Johnson.

Q. Out of all the shows you've done thus far describe what was your most memorable show and why?

A. My most memorable show was performing for 107.5 Shoes for Shorties with my old group because it was the first time I heard a crowd singing my lyrics back to me and that moment will always be cherished because in my eyes I was still just a normal guy.

Q. What was the name of the group you were in and why did y'all depart from each other?

A. Status Blak and we we're just another boy band that grew up and grew apart. Life hit us hard for a minute.

New Brand, New Movement

DESTINED TO BE A MAJOR PUBLIC FIGURE AND ACTIVIST, ON-AIR PERSONALITY JAMAL ALLEN SR. IS DETERMINED TO UNITE US ALL

by: Cheraee C.

Q. Describe your background in radio and how you got started...

A. Well, honestly my background in radio just started. I did an interview with Terry Martin from the Morning Toast Radio Show to promote the fashion show, The Vine Expo July 22nd where I'm going to be one of the featured designers for the show! After the show I told Terry how much fun it was doing radio and he got me in contact with the owner of CRB Radio. After an hour of us talking about my plans for a show and explaining to him about my United Us All movement, the rest was history!

Q. What made you want to focus your show on promoting unity and equality?

A. Well it goes hand in hand with my movement I started Unite Us All, a movement promoting unity and equality no matter your race, gender, or who you choose to love. There are also important issues such as depression and suicide awareness that aren't getting enough recognition in the world right now and I think it needs too.

Q. Tell us about some of the major areas your show will showcase and target, and what type of talents will be displayed, segments, and etc...

A. Unite Us All: The Show will do that, as well as showcase and recognize influential individuals in Detroit and the Detroit Metro Area that don't get the recognition they deserve. We also have fun segments like #LetsArgue, we have a segment called Poets Corner showcasing our talented poets. We showcase local artists once a month and have a whole show dedicated to them, and we also play music from your favorite artists!

Q. So you are a designer as well, what do you design and what's the name of your brand?

A. I design clothes, more specifically shirts. My brand/movement is called United Us All. The logo is UNITE in red, US in white, and ALL in blue, while the letters U.S.A are going connecting vertically down the shirt inside chain links. I used chain links because it represents togetherness and unity. I'm actually working on new designs and also working on doing pants and hats too!

Q. If your radio show could be on any radio network in the world, which one would you choose and why?

A. Honestly, I would stay with CRB Radio! They were the ones who gave me an opportunity to bring my show to life. I greatly appreciate that.

Based On A True Story

BEST-SELLING AUTHOR, PLAYWRIGHT, AND ALL AROUND ENTREPRENUER RASHELLE REY DISCUSSES THE GOOD AND THE BAD ABOUT HER STAGEPLAY
by Cheraee C.

Q. What made you want to turn your book I Am What God Says I Am into a stageplay?
A. Well someone talked .me into doing a stage play... I wanted to do a movie....so. I went on and pursued the stage play.

Q. Is your book and play based on a true story and give us a brief description of the storyline?
A. Yes the stageplay and the book are both based on a true story. A lot of the things and events that occurred through-out the play took place in my life. Some things and scenarios were exaggerated a little bit. The story is based on a young woman which is myself dealing with depression and sui-cidal thoughts from being molested. spending nights in the mental hospital .. Right here in Detroit on 8 mile.....Through Jesus Christ I was able to overcome a lot of those battles and because of him I was able to write the book and produce the stage play...

Q. What made you choose Detroit playwright Mark Hunter and his brand ReMarkable Productions to help you with your play?
A. I chose Mark Hunter because he is a excellent writer and he had a pretty decent name as far as the industry is con-cerned.

Q. What were things like working with Mark Hunter?
A. I was discouraged and I was played out of a lot of money. People took my testimony and made money off my story. I got overlooked. They took my story out of town and made money. I knew nothing about it....and I just felt like I didn't wanna do it because I felt that I paid money to get services and nothing was professional. Everything was a joke and my kindness was taken for weakness

Q. What are some of the lessons you learned from this pro-duction and what do you plan to do differently next time?
A. I learned that people will run you down take your money. Talk about how they took it. And I will tell anyone to make sure you know what's in your circle. Make sure they have in-tegrity, investigate the people you dealing with, and always let your light shine in the midst of wolves...It's a lot of pretenders that say they on the team. The best thing you wanna know is are you for the team or the come up....Next time go around I will move in silence and handle my own business instead of thinking I can trust people to handle it for me. And Keep my money to myself...I won't spend so free ly.

Q. How does it feel to have won the 2017 SDM Live Award for Best Stageplay of the year?

A. I am truly honored. I want to thank everyone that helped me with my vision especially Casino Bailey.

Q. You're going to be starring in a reality show. Tell us a little bit about it, and how you feel about this new venture?

A. I am so excited about the new reality show that will be hitting the TV stream real soon. I want people to see what stylists go through and the ups and downs of running a successful salon, and bringing a new twist to the city of Detroit.

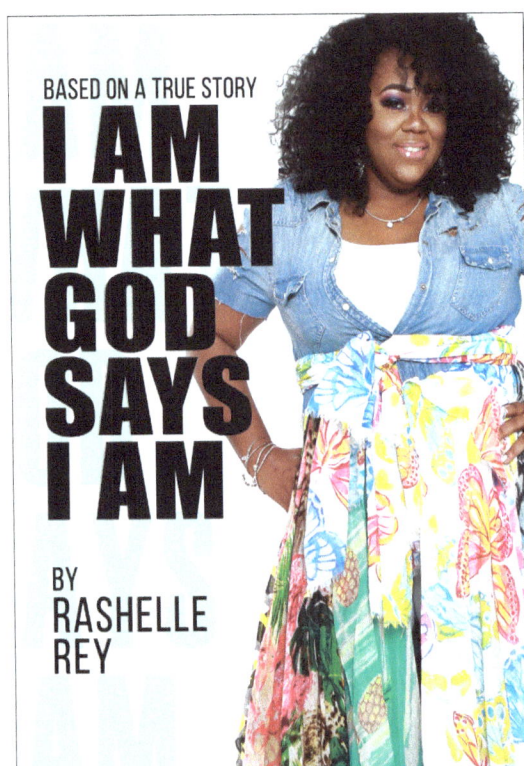

BASED ON A TRUE STORY

I AM WHAT GOD SAYS I AM

BY RASHELLE REY

The Sneaker Godz

FASHIONABLE CUSTOMIZED EAR-PLUGS, SNEAKERS, AND CLOTHING

by Semaja Turner

On October 21, 2016, across the US, a street fashion lifestyle brand was introduced, CEO, SneakerGod gave birth to SneakerGodz LLC. Within a xhort period of eight months, The Company has produced and expanded its own customized sneakers, clothing line, and Ear Plugs for many talented music artist and online retail platforms such as Raekwon, Lil Durk, and KarmaLoop. Also within this time period, Sneaker God has collaborated with Prophet Amen Ra, who currently handles strategic partnerships and celebrity relations for different brands. In doing so, Sneaker God appointed Prophet Amen Ra Brand Ambassador and Strategic Representative of the SneakerGodz Retro Plugs.

Prophet Amen Ra also controls the newest product concept-design, which serves as a new, alternative fashionable accessory while listening to the popular media content that streams right through your digital devices. Expanding the brand of The Retro Plugs, Prophet Amen Ra has been working hard when it comes to networking; booking interviews, advertising and setting meetings with many influential music artists. Public figures such as Big Tigger, Chanel West Coast, music journalist & television personality, Toure, Jordan River, Lil Bibby, Dreezy and Slim Jimmy from the hip-hop group Rae Surmmerd are all supporters of the Retro Plugs. With a cord length of 4ft and design material made of rubber, the Retro Plugs are replicas of your favorite, classic sneakers, and so far, the duo has created 5 different designs for your liking.

Big Things Popping

RAPPER JESUS ESKO IS ON THE VERGE OF NEW DISTRIBUTION DEALS AND SPEAKS ON HAVING TEMPORARY SETBACKS IN THE INDUSTRY

by Cheraee C.

Q. Since your last interview with SDM Live, what's been going on in Esko's world?

A. I been on the business side of the industry, but I had a few situations that delayed my project in terms of my mixtape release on a worldwide platform with major distribution.

Q. Would you like to reflect on these situations and how they affected your music?

A. It was mainly promo and distribution. The paperwork wasn't all the way together and this very moment we still putting it together so it's gone be a lil more time, but the wait is worth it.

Q. Are you signed to a new label? Is it fair to say you are in the works of something big and life-changing?

A. I can't speak on it at this moment I'm still in the middle of things. Yea we can say that. My music is relatable to a lot of people which allow them to have soundtrack to they life sort of speak, but it's motivating and life-changing for me so it favors both sides praise that lol.

Q. What's the secret on the connections you keep making? You always been a highly connected person…

A. The secret connection is connecting with myself praise that. People are drawn to my energy plus my creativity. I'm a believer that opportunity comes to those who attract it.

Q. How did it feel to perform at the 2017 SDM Live Awards and how do you feel about this SDM experience?

A. The awards was lit, I fucking enjoyed myself. I love the whole movement, it's a beautiful thing.

Two Plugs, One Vision

RETRO PLUGS SPOKESPERSON AND THE OBOV FOUNDER OF ONE BREATH,
ONE VISION JORDAN RIVER SPEAKS ON THE RETRO PLUG MOVEMENT

by No'el Snyder

Q. The video is amazing for your "Blow" intro, and without giving away too much, I noticed it had a double meaning towards your career. Can you elaborate and address the premises around the video?

A. What we wanted to capture was the fact I was in a state of mind where I felt trapped in a cycle, and I needed to find freedom so bad I had to blow up. (Metaphorically of course) but still destroying ANY wall of hating shit or those trying to deter me. Until the result being there's nothing left to stop me... I'm here alone thinking this way. In my own lane (or world even) my goal was when people look back there going to see all the signs that lead to me blowing up so I wanted to express that emotion in a metaphoric manner. I want people to look at my videos in the future and say he knew what he was aiming at way back then.

Q. How did you become a part of the retro plug movement? And are there any future plans for further expansion with the Retro Plugs?

A. I was first introduced to the Retro Plugs brand through Prophet Amen Ra. I heard whispers of it for about 2 months, but officially met SneakerGodz Shortly after finally seeing the headphones on a few celebrities. We spoke in-depth about the future, our careers, and expansion. We just had an organic conversation. It wasn't hard for me to see the vision. Were keeping them exclusive as we possibly can for now, by only allowing the culture movers and those of influence to have them; In addition, I have no official date when they'll drop for the public use. As far as what we're doing with my brand in correspondence with the 'Plugs' we recently upgraded equipment and have promotional videos, music videos (featuring the Retro Plugs), Interviews and overall just way more content. Perhaps in the future you might see a Jordan River x Retro Plugs collaboration item, you never know.

Q. When can fans get an initial release date for the "Blow" video? Can we hope for more visuals with the "Freedom" LP?

A. I actually do plan on dropping videos to Ballerinas, Honestly, and a few more very soon. As far as the blow video I can't give an official date but you can expect it sometime in September or October. It'll be worth the wait trust me,

Q. For your fans, you released a new song titled, "RAF (Remix)" on your birthday. What can we look forward to as far as future projects with music?

A. Yeah, Raf was the first track off of my No ceilings inspired Mini-project entitled: Wave 1. I felt since my birthday was the start to a new age I might as well start the new wave of music. What we're doing with the mini project is building the momentum for all the surprises we have dropping in October. You can look for Remixes too Magnolia, Free smoke, I might throw some Tupac in there, you never know lol.

Q. What skills/attributes you deem most important to existence being successful?

A. Well... I learned you really have to be emotionlessly consisting in this industry, that's one of the biggest things in our generation that breeds success. Someone who can move forward with blinders on without paying attention to the he say she says. Those are just distractions man, you have to know what you're going to do (plot it out) and as long as your executing moves that make sense to you. Why listen to the opposition that just leads to unconfident movements. This is chest when it comes down to it, "Consistency, Execution, and Focus".

TOP 10 CHARTS

TOP 10 DIGITAL SINGLES AND ALBUMS
SEMPTEMBER 1, 2017

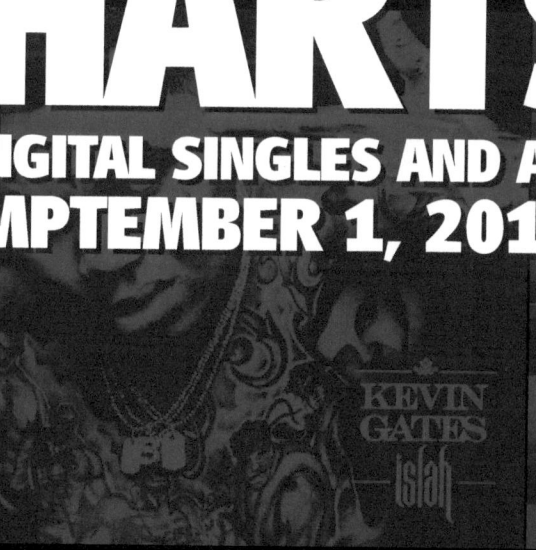

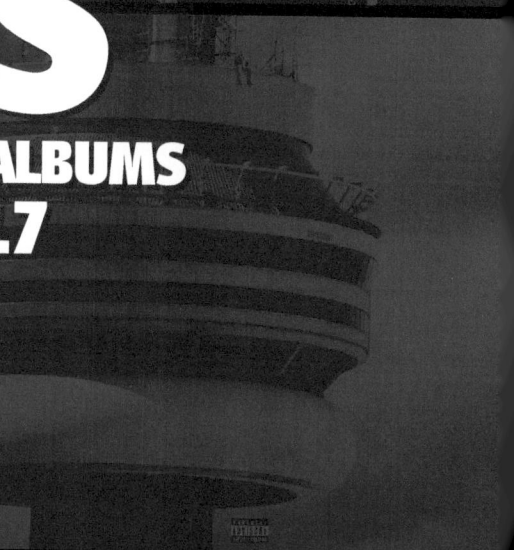

TOP 10 CHARTS

RAPPER CARDI B. DISCUSSES SUCCESS, HER NEW ALBUM AND THE TIME SHE MET BEYONCE.

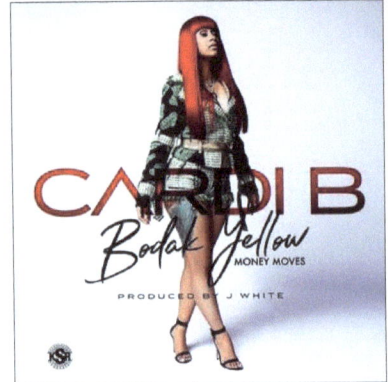

TOP 10 SINGLES
CHART OF THE MONTH

No.	Artist - Song Title
1	CARDI B. - BODAK YELLOW
2	DJ KAHLED - WILD THOUGHTS
3	FRENCH MONTANA - UNFORGETTABLE
4	KING DILLON - RIVALS
5	YO GOTTI - RAKE IT UP FEATURING NICKI MINAJ
6	JP ONE - MILLION
7	DEMI LOVATO - SORRY NOT SORRY
8	KHALID - LOCATION
9	21 SAVAGE - BANK ACCOUNT
10	LIL UZI VERT - XO TOUR LLIF3

TOP 10 ALBUMS
CHART OF THE MONTH

No.	Artist - Album Title
1	KENDRICK LAMAR - DAMN.
2	LIL UZI VERT - LUV IS RAGE 2
3	KHALID - AMERICAN TEEN
4	FUTURE - FUTURE
5	21 SAVAGE - ISSA ALBUM
6	BRUNO MARS - 24 CARET
7	DRAKE - MORE LIFE
8	DJ KHALED - GIFTFUL
9	MIGOS - CULTURE
10	2 CHAINZ - PRETTY GIRLS LIKE TRAP MUSIC

Sad For You
ARTIST: Njomza
RATING: 5

Pittsburgh native emcee, Mac Miller has a new addition to his "REMember Music" label, and I myself have grown very attached to her voice in such a limited amount of time. Njomza presents us with her debut EP "Sad For You". Production from Papi Beatz, Tommy Brown, Ryan, Caleb Stone & Mills, gave "Sad For You" a soul/pop Musical vibe; The intermixing of eighties resonance with strong, modern, low tempo RnB tunes that really complement Njomza voice. Tracks like "Perfect Fit", "Baggage", and "Poison" undoubtedly became my favorite songs on the EP, only because listening to the 22 year old song writer from Chicago, lyrically venting about how a love so strong can evolve into an addiction which was relatable for myself and others. Late nights will forever be recognized, when it comes down to discovering a new artist and great music and from start to finish, I truly enjoyed hearing & listening to Njomza. The production was utterly amazing and I have been searching for a music artist with a voice like Njomza's for quite sometime. I was overly excited that I stumbled upon her debut project. "Sad For You", was very empowering when the approach came to leaving a toxic relationship and being humble about it. The EP was about growing after a relationship has ended and wanting to show the other person that you've matured and that the reinvented you is now ready for that individual, giving them the best of you; The song "Hear Me" is a great example of that.

Y'all know that I know what good music sounds like, and I'm so appreciative of this artist for allowing an inside look into her life on such a personal level. I cannot wait until I hear your album! Check out Njomza's Debut EP "Sad For You" on SoundCloud and Spotify!

"See there's Consequences and Imperfections Sometimes, You Can't Come Clean of The Damage. So Stay Awake, You Should Pay Attention, It's Easy To Be Fooled."

Facing
ARTIST: Jaye Prime
RATING: 4

A perfect treasure of soulful melodies sung with passion, strength, and devotion. Jaye Prime, a music artist from Detroit, MI vocally shares her journey of growing into the creative woman she is today and her love & affection for marijuana. And as us listeners ride through the thick billow, with our windows rolled up, we can enjoy her 420 album release, "Facing". Read more… First and fore most, the title "Facing", in smoking terms means smoking alone. On March 28th, the 23 year old songstress gave birth to her musical project by releasing her highly anticipated single "Lemon-Aid". I myself was totally astounded with how crisp, strong, and endowed Jaye Prime's voice was, which led me to these 10 mellifluous tracks. The Production from Stacks Culture & Paradise with mixing and mastering done by Ashton Woods, included different drum kicks and a switch between electric & acoustic guitar; shout out to Adam and Robert Depollo. Giving inspiration to songs like "Nimbus", "Friend In Me", and "Hot Box" which included mixtures of those guitars, (acoustic guitar, electric guitar, and electric bass) offering a classical, subtle approach within Jaye Prime's lyrics. Other tracks like "Luna", "Way Up", and "Revovery" gave appreciation towards us nocturnal music listeners; the emotional atmosphere of a late night is definitely in the air. Inhaling that euphoric vibe, "Facing" is rapturously soulful, with gratitude for all the positive encounters that have blessed her throughout her life's journey. Combining Jaye Prime's blissful smoldering lyrics with the joyful production makes for a lovely project. "Facing" was more than just about smoking of course, releasing great music for us listeners to enjoy as we illustrate how we feel when we're listening! Always genuine vibes when it comes to this artist! Jaye, continue being a creator and constructing art! This album will continue to grow with me as I grow. Check out and listen to Jaye Prime's 420 album release "Facing" on Spotify, SoundCloud, and iTunes!

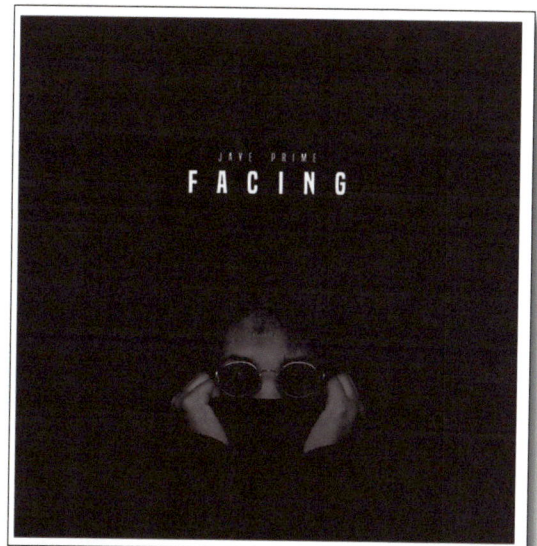

"I Come To You Cause I Can't Sleep At Night. My Heart Been Heavy, Give Every Piece of Me For Peace Of Mind. My Hand Been Steady, But I Can't Read the Words I Seem to Write Til I Saw That Burning Bush."

HEELS &
SKILLZ

Eron Blake
is a beautiful model
from Detroit, MI.

instagram
@LiYuantana

Photography by
@terancedrake

Ada Jones

is a model from
Detroit MI.

instagram
@modelmsadaj

HEELS &
SKILLZ

Photography by
@terancedrake

HEELS & SKILLZ

Unbeleivablee

A model in the movie True Religion from Detroit MI.

instagram
@_unbeleivablee_

Photography by
@barearmy

Cheraee's Corner

WHY ARE PEOPLE SO SELF-CENTERED WHEN IT COMES TO AWARD SHOWS?

by **Cheraee C.**

Why do people have to be winning or nominated for an award to be in attendance at an award show in their city? People should be more humble and supportive of these local award shows because it takes a lot of time, money. preparation, and dedication to orchestrate an award ceremony. People should be trying to network and connect with other artists instead of being competitive and showing poor sportsmanship. You never know how networking can impact your career. When has networking ever been a bad thing? People need to be more supportive of fellow artists and entreprenuers in their city because a lot of people are getting signed, making accomplishments, and have the potential to influence the industry.

Don't mess up your blessings by having a salty attitude and being self-centered. At the end of the day we are all winners.world. Black people can be so much richer, but not if we fail to be business-minded.

NEXT 2 BLOW

KAY JANEY

Q. What does your EP L.A.C.E stand for and when will you be releasing it?
A. There are a few meanings to my EP title L.A.C.E and what it stands for. Firstly, when you think of the material Lace, you think of something sexy right? Well at least I do, lol. All of the songs on this project will guarantee to put you in that mood. Secondly, going in order each song title will begin with the letters that spell out Lace. I was trying to be super creative with that, lol. Lastly, which is the most meaningful to me, this is my first project, my baby. I dedicate this EP to my daughter Lai'Cee. I call her LACE for short. She is my everything and I put my everything into this EP. I don't have an exact release date, but I do plan to have it released sometime in August.

Q. What do you dislike most about the females from our city in the industry today?
A. There's absolutely nothing that I dislike about the ladies doing their thing in the city. They inspire me more than anything. I love their grind. Their passion ya know. They are making more moves than ever. I do feel as if we should come together more and shake the city up a bit. I love my D-girls.

Q. What motivates your music the most?
A. I love this question! The motivation behind my music is the connection that it makes. Music is the one thing that brings us all together. I know for me personally, music has gotten me through some tough times when no one else was there for me. So if I can do that for someone else, get them through a difficult time just by my music alone, my job is done. It brings me joy when I can help someone while doing what I adore.

Q. Do you think it's harder to drop your first project or do you think future projects will be more challenging?
A. I think it's gonna be harder dropping my first project. I'm new to this so I'm still learning. It's a scary thing actually because I don't know what to expect. I'm wondering how will the feedback be. Will people feel my music? With future projects, I will have an idea of what the people want to hear and what they don't like so much. But, I'm excited to see how people react from my first project. I'm ready.

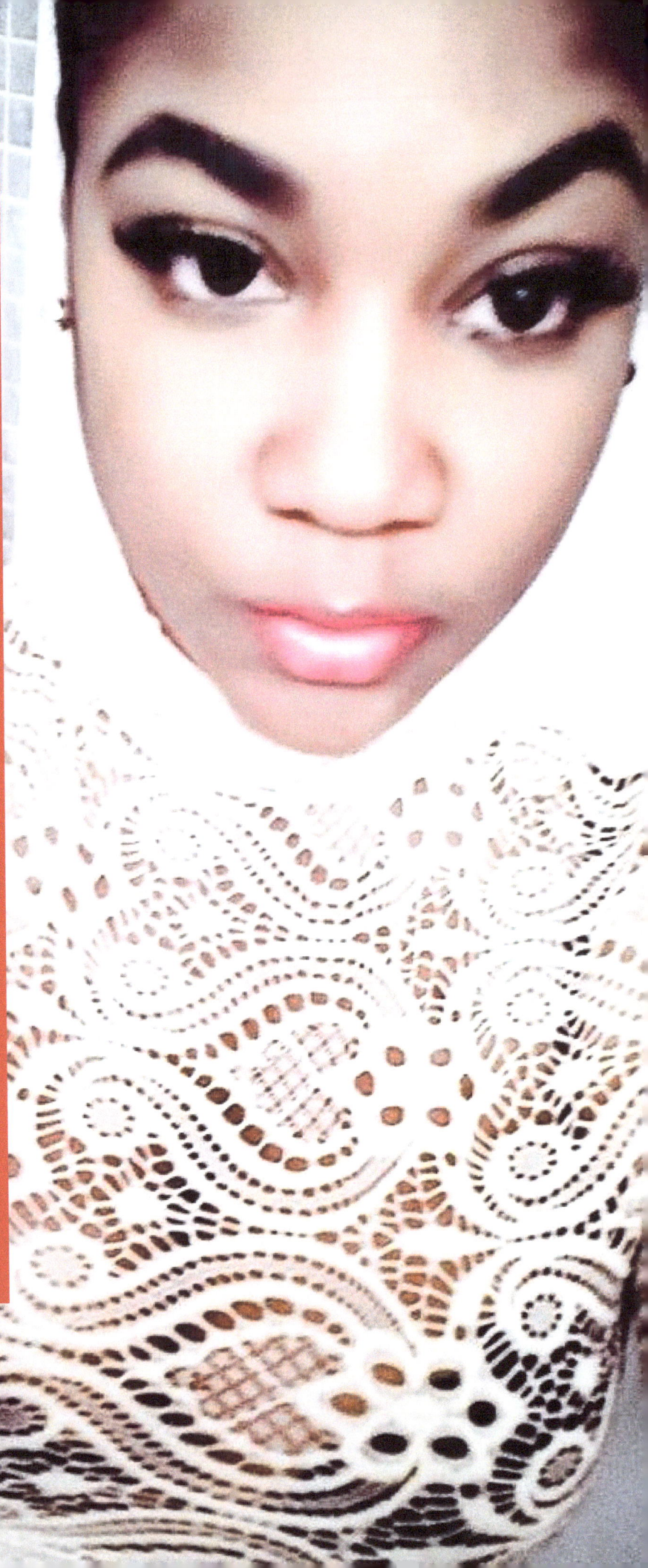

Q. How did you get involved with Convic Nation and in the music industry?

A. I've always known Convic "the person", we worked together in my teenager years lol. We just so happened to link back up as we were entering new chapters in our lives and careers. As for the music industry, I'm not really at the level I want just yet, but we're working on that lol.

Q. As an artist, what is your current biggest asset? What would you do without it?

A. My biggest asset is my mind! Without it I couldn't create the body of work that I am able to produce. I gotta say it is now and will always be my biggest and most prized asset!

Q. Who would you compare yourself to currently in the mainstream world and why?

A. I hate answering these type of questions because nowadays people try to use those comparisons against you. But if I did, I'd have to say Pharrell Williams aka "Pharrell" just due to the fact I'm comfortable making all types of music! Doesn't matter the genre, only how the music makes you feel! I like "6lack" too he's good.

Q. How does your daily life affect your music?

A. My music is affected by my daily life in all ways. How I live is affected in my music, what I see, what I feel. What you hear in my music is what I've lived through or going through now! I don't think my shit would be half as deep or emotion-felt if I didn't live how I do for real!

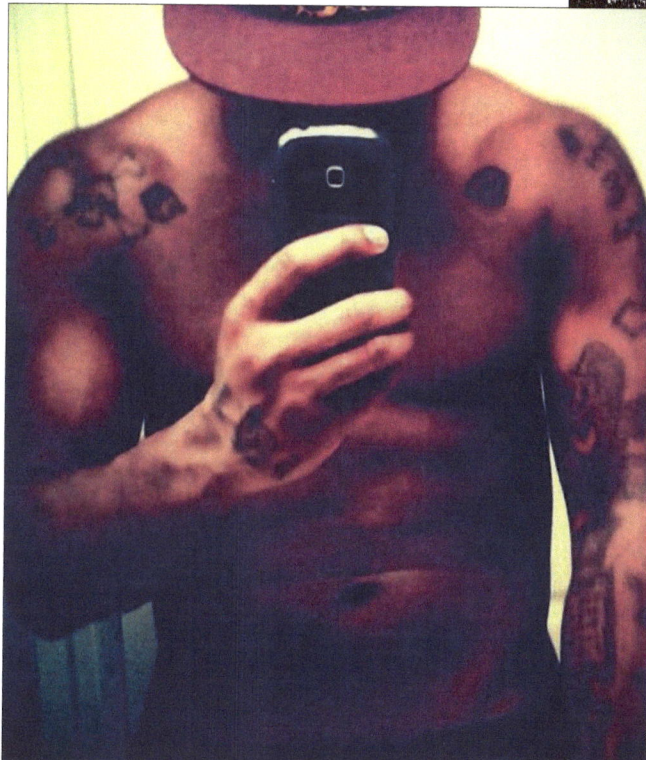

NEXT 2 BLOW
SHARIEK L'ZZZ

SNAP SHOTS

Email Your Snap Shots to
snapshots@sdmlive.com

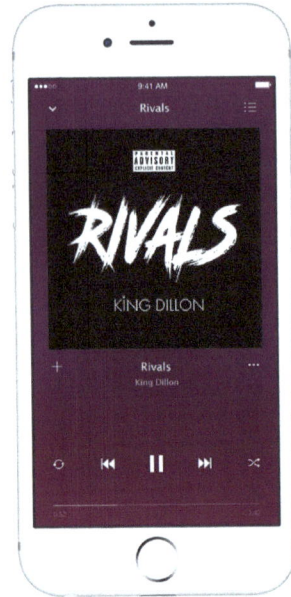

Urban Fiction, Spiritual, Motivation and more.
Order a book from Mocy Publishing today and receive FREE shipping.

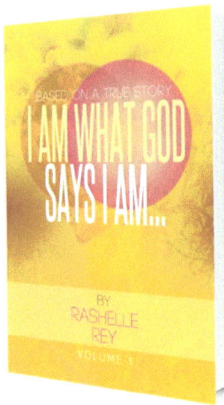

I Am What God Says I Am...
By Rashelle Rey

Item #: IAWGS29
Price: $9.99

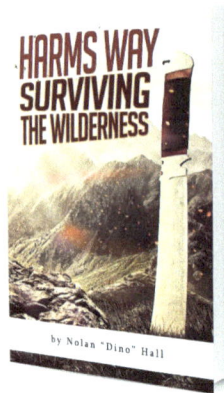

Harm's Way
By Nolan "Dino" Hall

Item #: HWS821
Price: $15.99

The Shadiest Mission Ever
By Cheraee C.

Item #: TSME28
Price: $12.99

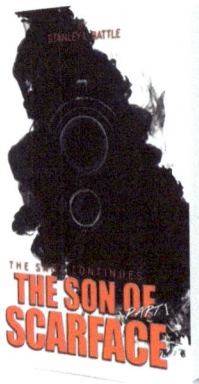

The Son Of Scarface – Part 1
By Stanley L. Battle

Item #: TSOS01
Price: $12.99

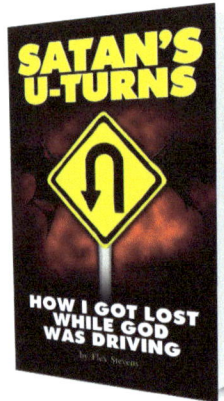

Satan's U-Turns
By Flex Stevens

Item #: SUT382
Price: $9.99

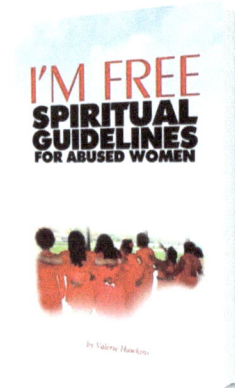

I'm Free
By Valerie Hawkins

Item #: IFTSG82
Price: $14.99

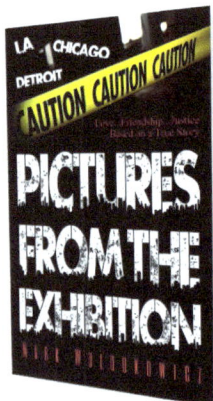

Pictures From The Exhibition
By Mark Wolodkowicz

Item #: PFAE292
Price: $15.99

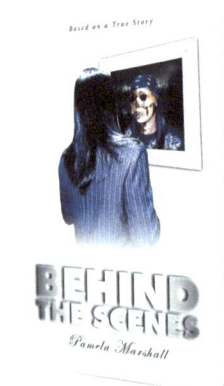

Behind The Scenes
By Pamela Marshall

Item #: BTS721
Price: $15.99

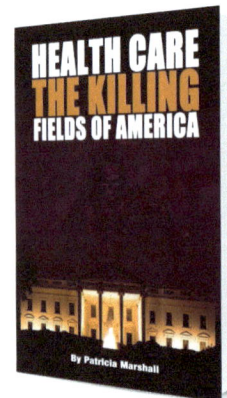

Health Care
By Patricia Marshall

Item #: HCTABF2
Price: $17.99

www.mocypublishing.com
order online and receive FREE shipping. Limit time offer.

From Behide The Wall

WINNING TWO AWARDS WHILE INCARCERATED IS SOMETHING PEOPLE
DREAM ABOUT, BUT NOT JP ONE AS HE COUNTDOWN THE DAYS TO FREEDOM
by JP ONE

What's good, SDM...It's JP ONE aka Jackpot Tha Chosen One aka Tha New Nigga You Love to Hate. I am currently incarecerated in Milan (Federal Facility). I don't talk much about my time, but if you really wanted to know it's not hard to find out. The thing about the Feds is there is good time, programs and half-way house programs that will put me out a lot sooner than the computer says, so technically you won't know when I'm coming home until I'm almost there. The case is none of everybody's business, but if you are a real fan, you heard the "R.I.C.O." song and watched the documentary on my website www.jponelife.com and YouTube. Basically, I am doing time for Conspiracy to Distribute Narcotics, though.

Although I have only been incarcerated a short period of time, I have been fighting this case for about two years. My closest family and friends were only aware of what I wanted them to be aware of, because the Feds play a totally different game. I have been reading a lot of business books and I'm getting ready to further my education by getting a business degree while I'm here. If you know me, you know I'm not one for wasting time. I want to thank everyone who has written me or emailed me and shown me love. If you are playing my music or sharing it on social media, I appreciate you. If you are acting like you are showing love to try to exploit my situation you will be held accountable. My fam is still my fam. I want to thank my lady, Lee Lee, and my niece, Layna Sky, for making sure my personal and business dealings are handled properly and my kids are taken care of. They are of the most importance to me. We are planning to continue to build the Gifted & Talented, LLC. brand by adding new team members and a few dope artists to the roster as soon as I return home.

We are continuing to build our network and ties within the music community in and outside of he city of Detroit. If you are trying to get in contact with me, you can message me via my personal and business FB pages and the information will be forwarded to me and a response will be delivered ASAP. You can also contact me directly via mail at:

Alvin C. Hill IV #51480039
4004 E. Arkona Rd.
Milan, MI 48160
#WESTILLWINNING

THE ALL NEW STYLE OF MAGAZINE-BOOKS